100 Limericks for 100 Days of Trump

PLUS
Limericks
from the
Other Side
of the
Aisle

SECOND EDITION

As Observed by
E. Reid Gilbert

A3D Impressions
Tucson | Minneapolis

100 Limericks for 100 Days of Trump

Copyright © 2017, 2018 E. Reid Gilbert. All rights reserved. No part of this book may be reproduced or retransmitted in any form or by any means without the written permission of the publisher.

Published by A3D Impressions
P.O. Box 57415, Tucson, AZ 85735
Cover/Art Direction: Donn Poll
Copy Editor: Dina Delaney
www.a3dimpressions.com
a3dimpressions@gmail.com

ISBN: 978-1-7320677-9-0
LCCN: 2018945104

Dedication

This collection of limericks is dedicated to Carie Graves, who urged me to put these daily scribblings in a book, and to all the other kids from Wisconsin to West Virginia, who have played and laughed with me over the frustrated silliness of life.

The Trump Drama
Cast of Characters

National Security Advisor FLYNN
Came to an early un-win.

Campaign Chairman MANAFORT
Tried to play the full court.

Attorney General Jeff SESSIONS
Carried earlier Civil Rights impressions.

Special Advisor Roger STONE
Threw Trump a political bone,

Campaign Manager Carter PAGE
In Moscow he was the rage.

Russian Ambassador KISLYAK
An international political hack.

Russian President Vladimir PUTIN
The role of a modern Rasputin.

The Limericks

1

To see the flesh of Michele's bare arms
Set the GOP into a state of alarm,
  But when Melania Trump
  Showed her bare rump,
'Twas just a thong of the Trump family charm.

2

Melania then connected in a new way
To Michele in her convention essay.
  When she realized
    She had plagiarized,
She had nothing further to say.

3

Mr. Trump's featured bodily size
Was noted by others so wise.
   Then one might wonder
   If in the down under
He may exhibit his October surprise.

4

Trump marvels at his own reflection,
Even after the questionable election.
  Ever since he was born
  He's tooted his own horn,
Lying being his prime predilection.

5

Permit us to be quite definite:
Our patience is certainly not infinite.
  Lies too often spoken
  And promises broken
His honesty is assuredly not in it.

6

The President-elect of our great nation
Dissed the "greatest actress of her
    generation".
  He's indiscreet
  About Meryl Streep
And has become a national irritation.

7

Washington loves throwing words around;
"Intelligence" is meant to astound.
   But to be quite direct
   Our president-elect
Demonstrates he has little to be found.

8

Olbermann says, "Trump's not quite there."
One may rightfully ask then where
  We might find
  One of his kind,
Somewhere primping his golden hair.

9

He ignores the official code of our flag
That when it becomes a soiled rag,
  It is discerned
  That it must be burned
And not subject to political brag.

10

Trump promised to build a Great Wall
Which must be fifty feet tall.
   The specs it must meet
   Will be reinforced concrete.
"Mexico will pay for it all."

11

We may instead erect a strong fence
Where population is not so dense.
   We'll employ guns anew.
   That we now must do.
Who knows what's in future tense?

12

He presented with great deliberation
His criticism of the previous administration,
  Even though Obama
  Rid the world of Osama
With Navy Seals in shared elimination.

13

Trump plans to adjust federal tax,
But he doesn't do well with the facts,
  That his exorbitant plans
  Will exceed the demands
Of the resultant lack of greenbacks.

14

When he says, "You must believe."
He has a joker up his sleeve.
  But the jokes on us,
  If we don't raise a fuss
When he attempts so oft to deceive.

15

That Putin is Trump's great pal
Is a blow to our national morale.
  Just let them both rattle
  In their shared saddle.
As together they enjoy their co-pal.

16

Of Narcissism Trump should be told
When the Greek god would behold
  At the water place
  To admire his own face,
He drowned when he lost his toehold.

17

All Muslims we must now deport
Great America is not for that sort.
  Their great sin
  Is to have darker skin
And to Mohammed they report.

18

800 jobs he promised to save
In the Great America enclave.
   But not to relax,
   Big heavy tax
For corporations who choose not to behave.

19

To make "America Great Again"
Was Trump's oft repeated refrain.
   Let's just hope
   The King of Grope
Will know which "swamp to drain".

20

Republicans want to repeal Obamacare.
We now have new mantras to declare
  That we must
  Plan to adjust
For the imminent ominous Trumpscare.

21

After Flynn had been officially hired,
In 18 days he was summarily fired.
   Though Flynn was dazed
   Trump still praised
Him in the Russian ploy that backfired.

22

At the time of the inauguration,
After a raucous contentious election,
  He continued to campaign
  Even in the rain
With his personal perpetual affectation.

23

Hoping for words of reconciliation,
We listened carefully to his oration;
  Wanting words to unite us
  Hearing words to divide us
Dashing our hopeful expectation.

24

To observe the work of a clown,
Brings a smile in lieu of a frown,
   But not the Grump
   We know as Trump,
Wearing a dunce cap instead of a crown.

25

My computer can't print P___ Trump.
For a solution I'm currently stumped.
  So let's get real
  And strike a deal
To regard the election as a mere bump.

26

Obama's message was, "Yes we can."
Trump answered with a "travel ban".
  Within a short time
  Without reason or rhyme
Negotiating is not in the Trump Plan.

27

Trump fired a woman named Yates.
She wouldn't bar the people he hates.
  Of course he thinks
  With a couple of winks
He's the Emperor of the United States.

28

Obama's choice for the Supreme Court,
McConnell refused to bring forth.
  Trump's choice of Gorsuch
  Wasn't very much,
But he expects the Senate's full support.

29

What's the significance of Standing Rock?
Perhaps a chance to enhance your oil stock.
Why do we heed
Such flagrant greed
When we pawn the Spirit to perpetual hock?

30

Ryan now says "repair" not "repeal".
Words at times are meant to conceal.
  But every chump
  Who voted for Trump
Should urge him his taxes to reveal.

31

"The most dishonest people in the world."
Was the epithet to the media he hurled
　As they continue to dig
　Though he says that it's rigged,
Even when his banner becomes unfurled.

32

When Trump pontificates "America first",
He seems to be well-versed
  In our egotism
  And his snobbism,
Implying other nations are the worst.

33

The truth is what "Trump says it is."
That's what he considers show biz.
   But when the curtain closes
   And he's grasped the roses,
The staged drama is no longer his.

34

The president touts the virtue of capitalism,
But turns it into an utter cataclysm
  In a national plot,
  Calling for a boycott
Against Nordstrom in a new McCarthyism.

35

McConnell commanded Elizabeth to desist
From revealing Sessions as a racist.
  He then did reveal
  And couldn't conceal
Himself as an actual misogynist.

36

McConnell complained, "She persisted."
We're happy Senator Warren "insisted"
　To tell the truth
　Though he was uncouth,
Exposing his motives so severely twisted.

37

"We hope the minority will treat the
     President with respect."
Is what McConnell asked us to accept and
     not suspect
  His leadership goal
  To have his minions enroll
To show President Obama utter disrespect.

38

"Persisted" was what McConnell whined,
Ignoring his own "persisting" byline
  To deprive Obama
  Of his own drama
And to cut short his presidential line.

39

What to do with Michael T. Flynn
For his call to Russia 'fore he was sworn in?
  He was an ingrate
  As in Watergate.
Will he be fired or will he stay in?

40

It's been three weeks but feels like years.
From Wall Street we hear loud cheers,
   Trump et al
   Wanted a wall
Prompting millions to quake in fear.

41

Responsible citizens would like to impeach
To correct the mistakes but not preach.
   Not even to score,
   But to restore
Sanity in the current political over-reach.

42

When the nation didn't applaud
Trump argued voter fraud.
   "There were millions
    Maybe even zillions!"
Not admitting his campaign was flawed.

43

Putin seems to be Trump's great pal.
They could write a wonderful musicale
  That together conspiring
  As Dems were expiring,
Sharing together a treacherous chorale.

44

This surely is a fertile political season
To look for an appointee who has reason.
　It's hard to know
　Which ones to throw
Under the bus to be charged with treason.

45

Security Advisor Michael T. Flynn resigns.
One may ask for whose political designs
  He'd have to go
  And dealt a death blow?
Surely he's ended his political assigns.

46

"Flynn is only the appetizer, Trump is the entrée."
Said intelligence agencies of the political fray.
   There'll be no more leaks,
   And whenever Trump speaks,
He confuses substantially the media repartee.

47

Now the question is, "Did Flynn act alone?"
Or was he just an available drone,
   To heed the call
   To carry the ball
And connect with Czar Putin via phone?

48

Can we trust Sessions to be transparent?
For many it would be quite apparent
   That the Attorney General
   Though rather ephemeral
Is a questionable political experiment.

49

What is this news of mafia connection,
Challenging Trump's view of his perfection?
　From his power
　In the Trump Tower
He regards Putin with great affection.

50

What are trans kids to do in this world
When their gender ID is atwirl?
   Trump says just see
   If you can find a tree.
But what to do if now I'm a girl?

51

McConnell advises from his box turtle
 syndrome
"Winners make policy; losers go home."
 But he shut 'er down
 When GOP lost the crown,
Vowing that Obama should be overthrown.

52

Trump wants our nukes to be "top of the pack".
An ensuing nuke race would jump off the track.
  Does no one realize
  There will be no prize?
But a gift to the world from our megalomaniac.

53

We mustn't allow ourselves to equivocate
When an official advisor preaches racial hate.
  Like Steve Bannon
  A loose cannon
Running amok on our national ship of state.

54

What a frightful ogre Morning Joe
You've unleashed on your morning show?
  A frightful freak
  With a fascist streak
But Trump gives Miller a presidential Bravo.

55

There's still the issue of a Trump-Russia contact.
Will they yet hide behind an alternative fact?
And by the by
A lie is still a lie,
Even when Trump is devoid of presidential tact.

56

Trump's as stubborn as a dadburn mule.
He's now reinstated the global gag rule.
  No further action
  For the female faction;
Providing for women's health is officially uncool.

57

It was true that General Flynn
Assumed he was definitely in.
  At first he trumped
  And then was dumped,
With a loss instead of a win.

58

And then there is Senator Sessions
With his previous racist obsession.
   And Vice-President Pence
   Tried to make sense
Of his own far right regression.

59

Sessions was sitting on a hot seat.
His views had certainly been indiscreet.
　He was caught,
　So he thought
He'd recuse with a hasty retreat.

60

Though Trump did rave and rant
His appointees would not recant.
   But they hit the wall
   With "I don't recall."
Amnesia became quite rampant.

61

Pence and others did critically assail
Hillary for using her private email.
  It was revealed hence
  That Governor Pence
Used also detail of private email.

62

Our nations had dispensed with kings and czars
With our respective revolutionary wars.
  We're there again
  And monarchy doth reign,
Trump and Putin with their narcissistic empires.

63

Trump's oft-quoted political refrain,
"To make America great again,"
   Is to go back
   But exposes a lack
Of any hope for new meaningful gain.

64

Trump announced with usual gesticulation
That it could be "a very serious situation,"
  When he rapped
  That he's been tapped.
It was just his latest prevarication.

65

The White House is trying to explain
Trump's baseless wire-tapping claim;
  Perhaps a little shy
  Of an outright lie,
But the explanation was certainly lame.

66

Donald Trump is unabashedly uncouth.
We've endured his bluster forsooth.
   It would be nicer
   If Sean Spicer
Would himself tell the whole truth.

67

"He was very clear, he was very broad."
The contradiction left me strangely awed.
   Depend on Sean
   To miss it dead-on
Dancing around the issue we would applaud.

68

Washington's in a terrible mess
Health issues under much duress.
  We tried to share
  With Obamacare
Till replaced with TrumpCareLess.

69

Now with an office in the West Wing
Ivanka prepares to do her thing;
  Whatever it is
  Even classified show biz,
She'll be helping Daddy, the King.

70

A year ago was Obama's nominee.
McConnell was a partisan absentee.
  But now it seems
  The GOP deems
Gorsuch must be confirmed ASAP.

71

Investigating the crude business man
Over a long several months span,
   But Comey had to pounce
   In October to announce
As soon as Hillary's investigation began.

72

Spicer informs us there's no Plan B
To repeal Obamacare, but we'll see.
  Alas, poor Sean
  Is so put upon,
He may have to announce Plan Z.

73

It appears much more than evidential
The circumstance of Trump's collusion
  With Putin's plan,
  But a demand
To know what now is the conclusion.

74

The committee was all a fluster
And Trump as usual did bluster.
　They wanted so much
　To confirm Gorsuch.
Schumer threatened to filibuster.

75

"I'm through negotiating the health bill."
Was Trump's message to the Hill.
   But if it should fail
   No more blackmail,
And Obamacare will be with us still.

76

Of Obamacare Trump did complain
That "The democrats are to blame."
　He flipped his rug
　When he pulled the plug;
Other republicans wouldn't play his game.

77

Trump is mightily dismayed;
Healthcare is greatly disarrayed.
  But O how sweet
  Is the tweet
When he says, "Be ye not afraid."

78

Congress has become supine
When appointments miss the deadline.
  But there isn't a show
  By the party of NO,
As Trump finishes playing the back nine.

79

Trump's aim is to finally negate
Obama's action on our climate,
  To revert back to coal
  And if truth be told
All such progress to eliminate.

80

He now sends his son-in-law
Abroad with hopes to declaw
  Uprisings in Iraq
  Ignoring his lack
Of experience in international law.

81

Whimpering Trump has stated
"Health care is so complicated."
   We must be aware
   That Trumpcare
Proves to be much over-rated.

82

Trump would dispense with NEA
To use funds in another way.
  Some guns
  Would be fun
We'll play music another day.

83

Trump should confide with the taxpayer
That healthcare is like the card player.
  Play the ace
  Putting in place
The highest card being the single payer.

84

What to do about climate change?
Trump would prefer an interchange
　Of scientific facts
　With coal contracts
So mountaintops could be a rifle range.

85

It now appears that Bannon is out.
He did delight his power to flout.
   But who did win
   And is now in?
Kushner is apparently now Head Scout.

86

Canada lures tech jobs up north
As Trump's policies spew forth.
  His proclamation
  For immigration,
Scaring everyone now and henceforth.

87

What's the deal with Carter Page?
It seems he actually did engage
  On the fly
  As a spy
For Russia and was paid a fat wage.

88

Manafort's secret Russian contact
Gave him a ten million dollar contract.
  In this post-Obama
    Comic drama
We wait for the final tragic act.

89

"I have here in my hand . . . "
Was McCarthy's initial stand
   Of accusations
   And fabrications;
Quite similar to current Trump brand.

90

Politics inspire some interesting prose.
New words in our lexicon arose.
  The word BROMANCE
  Means the NEW ROMANCE
Of Trump and Putin NARCISSISTIC BROS.

91

Dr. Carson says, "Poverty is a state of mind."
I remind him and others of his kind
  That the incubators
  Of poverty haters
Are fueled by greed, leaving compassion behind

92

Trump's words with ironic profusion
Caused much misleading confusion.
  He thus did admire
  Putin and conspire;
Both accused now of collusion.

93

Nichols's "One Hundred Days of
    Resistance"
Includes appointees with their malfeasance.
  To "derail the Trump train"
  We recall once again
Elizabeth Warren's insistent persistence.

94

Trump didn't win in the Obamacare fight,
And discovered "healthcare is a right".
  Now the addenda
  Of our agenda
To provide resistance ere a political night.

95

"The New McCarthyism of Donald Trump"
Simon Jenkin writes about our chief grump.
  The McCarthy age
  Is our new page
When Trump considers everyone a naive chump.

96

Trump says Muslims are to blame.
McCarthy fostered this folkish claim,
  "A red
  Under every bed."
Trump continued Obama to defame.

97

What happened to traditional political debate?
We have lost the means to communicate.
  Instead of clarity
  We get vulgarity
From Trump who sees himself as the high potentate.

98

The fear in our past was of a national oligarchy.
Have we settled instead for a billionaire monarchy?
As of this day,
I'd just like to say,
"His pronouncements are just inane malarkey."

99

How could we hope to remove Trump from office
When already considered an unspeakable orifice?
  In my opinion
  His naive minions
May succeed to dethrone the unspeakable riche.

100

During Trump's first 100 days
With absolute political malaise
  It became apparent
  Forget transparent;
He's enshrouded in a slough of self-praise.

Limericks from the Other Side of the Aisle

Hillary's political climb was uphill
She'd had to deal with her Bill.
   Even after Monika
   Played the harmonica
Hillary as always is with Bill still.

Hillary hoped to be the first female
To open the presidential email.
    With a great deal of Hope
    She set her telescope
But that ship of state didn't sail.

Clinton pursued his agrarian powers
Hunting game in a multitude of bowers.
   His libido took flight
    With a healthy appetite,
And collected 12 years' worth of Flowers

Bill came from a little burg named Hope
The political scene widened his scope.
   His roving eyes
   Prompted some lies
As he walked an impeachment tightrope.

Hillary was anxious to be head of state.
She hoped her talents would predominate,
   But her Benghazi,
   Not exactly a kamikaze,
But enough to seal her political fate.

A Democratic Congressman named Weiner
For the camera was a preener.
   But the shots
   Of the crotch
Became Weiner's misdemeanors.

And then there was Senator Bernie
Much more than a mere attorney;
   To our surprise
   Rallies of great size
But Hillary finished Bernie's political journey.

www.ingramcontent.com/pod-product-compliance
Lightning Source LLC
Chambersburg PA
CBHW060458080526
44584CB00015B/1474